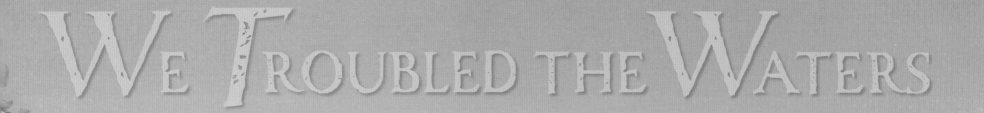

WE TROUBLED THE WATERS

Poems by **Ntozake Shange**

Paintings by **Rod Brown**

Amistad ⬤ Collins

An Imprint of HarperCollinsPublishers

I dedicate this book to my wife, Cathy Brown, who said to me:
"We troubled the waters when God's great hand came down and stirred us."
—Rod Brown

I would like to thank the following people:
Mrs. Srisucha B. McCabe, Mr. Charles S. Amorosino, Jr.,
Claudia Menza, and my editor, Ms. Phoebe Yeh.
—Rod Brown

Amistad and Collins are imprints of HarperCollins Publishers.
We Troubled the Waters
Text copyright © 2009 by Ntozake Shange Paintings copyright © 2009 by Rod Brown Manufactured in China. All rights reserved. No part of this book
may be used or reproduced in any manner whatsoever without written permission except in the case of brief quotations embodied in critical articles and
reviews. For information address HarperCollins Children's Books, a division of HarperCollins Publishers, 10 East 53rd Street, New York, NY 10022
www.harpercollinschildrens.com
Library of Congress Cataloging-in-Publication Data
Shange, Ntozake We troubled the waters : poems / by Ntozake Shange ; paintings by Rod Brown.— 1st ed.   p.   cm. ISBN 978-0-06-133735-2 (trade bdg.)
— ISBN 978-0-06-133737-6 (lib. bdg.) 1. African Americans—Poetry. 2. Racism—United States—Poetry. 3. Race discrimination—United States—
Poetry. 4. African Americans—Civil rights—Poetry.   I. Brown, Rod, date. II Title. PS3569.H3324W4 2009 2008025360 [811'.54]—dc22 CIP AC
Designed by Stephanie Bart-Horvath 09 10 11 12 13 SCP 10 9 8 7 6 5 4 3 2 1 ❖ First Edition

To the Little Rock Nine with great appreciation.
—Ntozake Shange

BOOKER T. WASHINGTON SCHOOL, 1941

was only one room for all the eager

brown faces / hair braided neatly or parted

down the side / the black and brown children

had faith this day / why less than a century ago

they'd have hung or burned alive /

for learning to read and write

but thanks to Booker T. schools for our

children were sprouting up every which way

& teachers from Tuskegee were not only on

their way / but pledging to have each black child

know how to spell her name "m-a-t-t-i-e

j-o-h-n" sure nough be able to vote one day

imagine one day the world at their fingertips through

language / up ye mighty race challenged Marcus Garvey

and 'long with their victory gardens / our children

were ready to grow

EAGER TO LEARN

bright eyes / books in hand
they simply want a place to learn
but who'll take two little negro girls
they're no danger / no threat
why threaten they right to learn

CLEANING GAL

if they catch me sittin / jus' for a moment
i might lose this heah job / but i can't 'ford to do that
all my children / matt, maceo, bertha, mae, sunshine, and the baby
'long with ma / look to me for vittles and shelter /
it's just that i got to scrub all these floors till they'd look like glass /
that takes all day and i still aint got to the laundry yet /
boilin clothes / starchin shirts /
Lawd have mercy i got to spend all day tomorrow ironin
so the missus and her mate can go to some bigshindig /
sposin i quit / how we gonna eat / no i aint goin nowhere /
& there aint no fancy duds or dancin in my future /
just scrubbin & scrubbin what aint mine

GARBAGE BOYS

sometime there's bone with meat
left on em / or a day-old biscuit
steeped in butter or honey /
best be careful not to cut
yourself / glass down there too
never understand / how folks
throw way what's still good
to eat / expect we gonna fill
these pails with old dry leaves
fore we feed our stomachs

WATER FOUNTAINS

it's lucky for them
they could read
"colored" & "white"
signified who could
drink water from where
they were a bit puzzled
it was just water
but it was against the law
to get confused & have the
white boy drink from the
colored or the colored drink from the white
a serious crime under Jim Crow

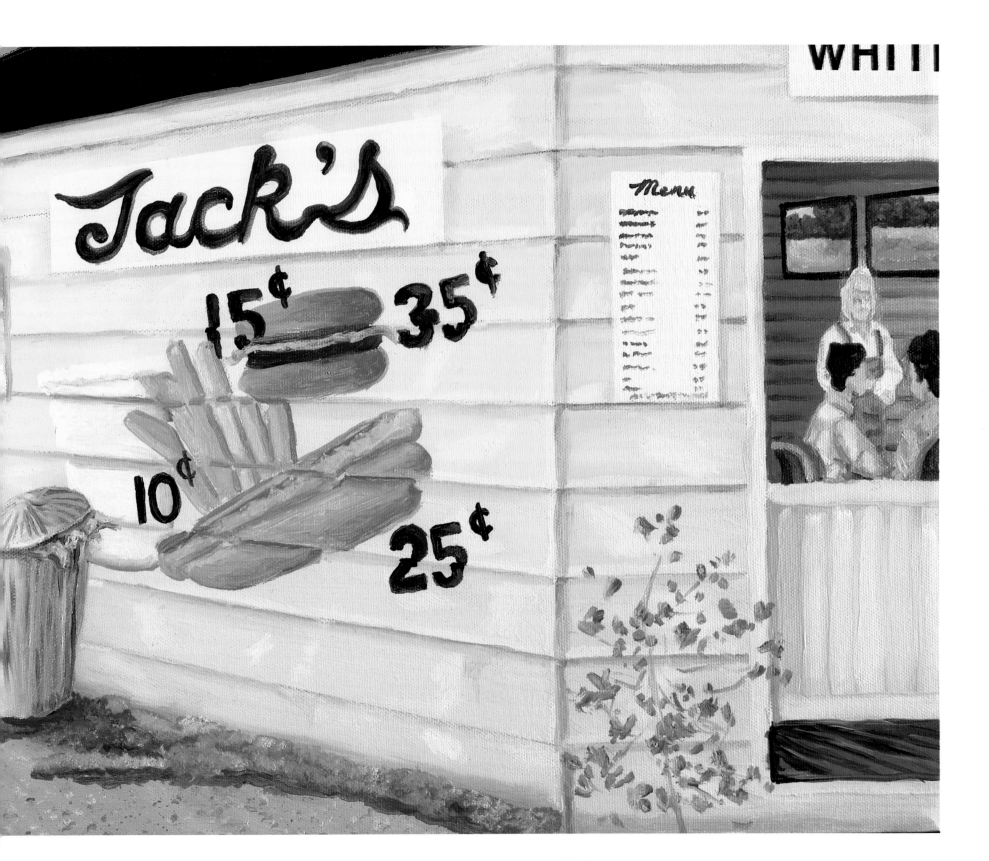

WHERE I LIVE

call them shotgun houses
cause you could shoot straight
through them / got 13 folks livin
here / a good gas-burnin stove /
wasn't always like that / papa says usedta
be wood / & handmade quilts kept us warm /
now we got newspaper on the walls
to keep out the drafts / and mousetraps for
other things / found a special place for me
to sleep / right neath the kitchen table /
ever so warm & smellin so good /
great-grandma got the best bed / the rest
of us share like we do everything / no time for fightin
ma says the world is cruel enough must always keep
some lovin at home / no matter how folks look
at us / we still a family

CRYING TREES

the throng of heavy boots crumblin /
dry leaves dimpled with blood and sweat
has disappeared / only now God looks upon
the work of humans gone toward Satan's
door / some mothers' sons peek through
the landscape of cruelty and vibrant green
confusin us / playin tricks with our
senses / how can our boys be some
decorations in the forest / never to kiss
good night again / never to hold other
sons in their arms again / cut em down now
if we dare / how long are we to gaze on our gifts
taunting the loveliness of livin / cut em down

ROADKILL

when we are round

each other / gramma uncle joe susie

and mack / we people / we folks

laughin & chattin / talkin bout old times

out there in the night

alone

we aint nothin

we aint people

we animals

roadkill

YOU VOTE / YOU DIE!

we go to vote & the white folks laugh
"you own land round here?" "who were the last
20 presidents?" "who was the head of the
confederacy?" "you mockin the confederacy
of these united states?" "count backward from 100"
"can you read and write?" or your mark'll have to do
after that somebody finds a body
"you vote / you die"

THE KU KLUX KLAN

for generations they terrorized us
burned crosses houses bodies and marched
into the night to bring fear to the front door
of any & every negro / their meetins were
circuses with cakes and candies / and someone hangin
from a noose / the cowardice was obvious / could be
the banker / the butcha / the mechanic / all covered
in white so no one knew who they were / they
took no responsibility for the heinous reign
of death they dealt / hatred dies hard
death & the Klan aint dead yet

THANK YOU ROSA PARKS

bastin stitches runnin stitches

hemmin stitches cotton pickin cuttin cane

nursin babies standin in the back of the bus

we were all there

whether the white section in the front

was empty or not

thank you Rosa Parks

for sittin down cause you was tired

& they handcuffed you & dragged you away

cause you were tired, dear Rosa Parks

you were all of us who are tired

of beatins, fires, police & havin

nowhere to rest

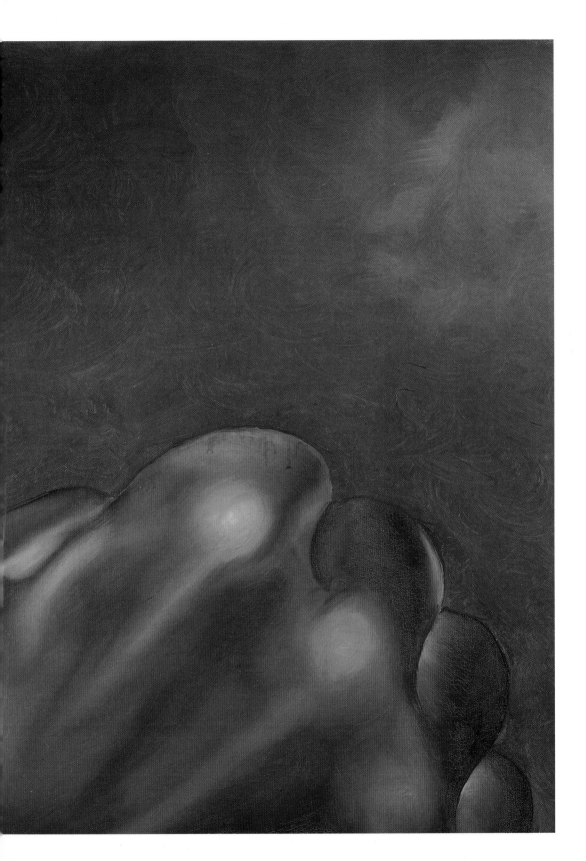

MARTIN LUTHER KING, JR.

millions of denigrated / humiliated negroes / without
enough food / land / schools / or shoes always walkin
in fear / walkin out of the way of white folk / or
the watch of the KKK / who could be the butcha
the judge / the fireman / whisperin to each
other / fearin their dreams meant / death
heard a rousin young voice outa Birmingham
sayin stand up / you got a right to
be American / stand up and morally challenge
those who seek to keep you crawlin on
your knees / Martin Luther King brought a
faith and fight to the negroes who'd been
cowed / knowin full well "i might not
get there with you" / & he did not / but
his spirit of belief and nonviolence
carried the rest of us onward / out of the
darkness / out of peonage / & into dignity

BROTHER MALCOLM

his recruits / convicts / addicts / prostitutes
not church ladies with big hats & gardens
Malcolm found a garden of black folks
in the throwaways of the negro & called
the white man / the devil which many
believed already / he told us we'd been
lied to / we weren't joneses calhouns and
williamses / those were slave names / hence "X"
the Fruit of Islam was there to protect us / not the cops
the Nation of Islam was there to prepare us
to take care of our own / not Safeway / it was the
ballot or the bullet / Malcolm wasn't
playin / he prayed on his knees only before
Allah / he didn't give a damn what a
white man thought of him

SITTIN DOWN IS STANDIN UP

'long with the aroma of hot dogs
& burgers / was the stench of venom
& hatred / the cowardice of many gainst
a few / their arms this time / broken eggs
smeared tomatoes / mustard & ketchup
just to let us know / we weren't welcome to
eat at the five & dime / or anywhere else
a **WHITES ONLY** sign held sway / we sang
spirituals / and held our heads high / till the
cops came to take us away / trespassin / they say
but more of us will / till the **WHITES ONLY**
signs come down

AND WE MARCHED

we took the children / women /
teenagers & elders / hand in hand
& we marched / from the blessed steps
of the churches to the doors of city hall
we marched
we marched through water hoses
past snarlin dogs / under nightsticks
and just out the sights of rifles
but we marched
we marched cause freedom buses burned
we marched cause cars disappeared
we marched cause this is our land too
was time somebody knew

THE PRAY-IN

they were standin with nightsticks & guns

ensurin peace

at a pray-in

like the might of God

was gonna strike them down / kneelin

hats in hand / humble and white & black together

they were wrapped in faith and the

knowledge that God looked after

his children even in the face of Caesar

or Bull Connor

Bull Connor was a police official in Birmingham, Alabama, who authorized the use of fire hoses and attack dogs against protesters. A member of the Ku Klux Klan, Connor was an open supporter of racial segregation and became a symbol of racism and bigotry in the 1960s.

LORRAINE

calm evening / one blarin shot outa nowhere

who knew that Lorraine would not just be some

girl's name / but a memory burnin in the souls of millions

Andy Young / Ralph Abernathy / conjurin up the sermon

the night before / Martin claimin "i might not get there with you"

and then the shot

the gut-wrenchin cries the nation afire

rage & love underestimated

we pleaded for nonviolence / they didn't listen

& the cities went crazy

Martin oh Martin

On April 4, 1968, Dr. Martin Luther King, Jr., was assassinated outside the Lorraine Motel in Memphis, Tennessee. The National Civil Rights Museum was opened at this site on September 28, 1991.

HEAH Y'ALL COME

now the children run freely
toward each other
knowin no fears of the other
so what? she's brown and her lips thick
so what? yarmulkes atop their heads
Buddha's smile graces their faces
now America welcomes all the babies
sí sí / todos los niños are ours
yes yes / wa alaikum salaam
& the gods watch over all children
& the flag protects each American
all